Above the Forests

RUTH BIDGOOD

INDEPENDENT INNOVATIVE INTERNATIONAL

Published by Cinnamon Press
Meirion House, Glan yr afon, Tanygrisiau
Blaenau Ffestiniog, Gwynedd, LL41 3SU
www.cinnamonpress.com
The right of Ruth Bidgood to be identified as author of this work
has been asserted by her in accordance with the Copyright,
Designs and Patent Act, 1988. Copyright © 2012 Ruth Bidgood
ISBN: 978-1-907090-66-0

British Library Cataloguing in Publication Data. A CIP record for
this book can be obtained from the British Library.

Designed and typeset in Palatino by Cinnamon Press
Cover from original artwork 'Gospel Pass' by David Martin
Hughes © Agency: dreamstime.com
Cover design by Jan Fortune

Printed in Poland

Cinnamon Press is represented in the UK by Inpress Ltd
www.inpressbooks.co.uk and in Wales by the Welsh Books
Council www.cllc.org.uk

The publisher acknowledges the support of the Welsh Books
Council

Acknowledgements

Some of these poems first appeared in the following magazines-

Cambria, Interpreter's House, London Grip, New Welsh Review, Planet, Poetry Scotland, Poetry Wales , Roundyhouse, Scintilla.

'Set Free' appeared in the Cinnamon anthology, *Kaleidoscope.*

Contents

The Copy   9
Recall   10
A Good Day   11
Forests
    1. Above the Forests   12
    2. Windblow   14
    3. Hayfield   15
    4. New Spell   16
    5. Wild Sheep   17
Lit Room   18
The Will   20
The Ram   22
Joy   23
Woodpecker   24
Dreams
    1. New Year Dream   25
    2. Landmark   26
    3. Threshold   27
    4. Pale House   28
Threat   29
Bridges   30
Treachery   32
Capel-y-Ffin Story   33
Genealogy
    1. Census   34
    2. Black Elm   35
    3. Gone Wrong   36
    4. Compulsion   37
Butterflies at Wellfield   38
Garlanding the Urn   39
Eyes   40
Time and the Running Child   41
Swallow Leaving   42
Homecoming   43
Wrecker and Roaring Saint   44
To the Fish Traps   46

Set Free

    1   47

    2   48

    3   49

    4   50

    5   51

Looms   52

All Manner of Thing   53

Rainbow   54

Dance   56

Wind in Sumac   57

Diptych, Generation Gaps

    1. Before the Dark   58

    2. Reading Yeats in September   60

Driving Home   61

At Capel-y-Ffin   62

Birds Returning   63

Elan in Autumn   64

Rhaeadr Castle   65

October Light   66

Links

    1. Entanglement   67

    2. Weather Forecast   68

    3. Linked   69

Film Ending   70

Bethlehem   71

More of the Same   72

Harmony   73

Tout Passe   74

House By The Ford

    1. Noon   75

    2. Picnic   77

    3. The Glade   78

Notes   80

To the people of Abergwesyn,
past, present, to come

Above the Forests

The Copy

Scribbled on the back,
Valley near the dam.
An unremarkable photograph,
pleasant enough, born of a wish to record
even the less distinctive
dips and summits on the fringe
of a happy afternoon.

It's the copy that went wrong
astonishes, illuminates.
An accidental overprint
shows on the right, tip-tilted,
a sharply-angled block of darker shades,
weirder light – an inversion
of bush and fern, seeming lit from below,
unearthly beneath a discoloured sky
that's upside-down hill.

It's taken a botched anomalous image
for me to see the strangeness here, the sharp
uneasy shapes half-masked
by branch and grass; to celebrate
a dark perturbing beauty –
and sense again the brush of shadow
over laughing hours.

Recall

It seems important
to remember right:
know exactly the angle
of house to hill, be able
to count the pines
in their protective line,
to picture the shape
of that pallid lichen-patch
on a rock by the spring –

as though the intensity
of my recall
ensured the reality
of the place, its being,
no longer seen, but there,
undoubtedly there; as though
if I forgot one stone, one gleam
of sun on windowpane, one
rusty bar of the skewed gate,
all would not only have gone,
but never have been –

as though the existence
of a loved place were something
to be built, sustained
each moment, held to, against
the cold and cancelling wind.

A Good Day

You were driving with the wrong man
into the wrong city, but still
remember it as a good day.
                                    Any city
can be a promise – this one sprawled ahead,
away and away, into the mystery
of its brumous exhalations,
and a young year's weak sun.
                                    Behind you
the road curling down out of low hills,
the opulent suburb up there, its pond
under budding trees – ducks, even,
remember?
                    Happiness was never
going to be part of the mix, but there were
good days. Those drop, one by one,
their light weight on to the balance,
tiny stones with a faint undeniable shine.

Forests

1. Above the Forests

Across the valley, in the forest,
is a felled square, striped
with new planting. In squads, platoons,
battalions, the trees march
to their abrupt death. Soon
cleared slopes bristle
with the new young levy.

If you knew what was there,
or the day's chance went your way,
deep in the grown forest
you might find the memorial,
waymark, prayer-stone(who knows which?) –
an ancient stillness, greyness,
enigma, always a survivor, always
on its way back into hiding.
                              Or you might
just miss a cut from rusty chunks
of corrugated roof, propped on dark roots
upheaved by a windblow, and have enough
scraps of rumour to recognise
what's left of a dead farm.

Climbing to a track above the forests,
you can see the far, bare,
untouched hills at the valley's head.
If sun is shining, it will seem
they could never be dark; it will seem
your youth is there, and your future,
saved. You'll remember that,
when the rain sweeps over,
or when the north-east blows;

when you touch conglomerate rock
glaciers bore down; when for a moment
you can feel the nothingness
of a million years; when all that seems real
feels like a beginning.

2. Windblow

The forest road edges down
along a gulf of mist, through a demesne
of misrule. Huge clods of earth,
sprouting whiskery roots, teeter
on the verge of nothingness.

In chill unstirring air
battered conifers lean where they crashed
against mutilated survivors.
Green litter of fallen branches
half-hides limbless trunks.

In misty clearings, diggers, forwarders
gleam yellow – purposeful amid
the mess of trees brought low.

By the roadside, long walls
of fir-poles, close packed, row on row
lie ready for carrying – as if
the wind were instrument only,
and this a plan's fruition,
the outcome always known.

3. Hayfield

The hay had gone over that year –
and how many others? Seeded grass,
still beautiful, rippled in a hot
late-summer wind.

Since my sixties' photographs
from the opposite hill,
the forests had grown, flanking with dark
the track to the broken house,
closing round the yard, sheltering
small unfamiliar plants, that had joined
moss and lichen to enrich
the unvisited glade.

           I remembered
taking those pictures one spring –
mile on stubbly mile of new planting
bristling over the hills.
           And amongst all that,
high up, one pale clearing unplanted –
the old hayfield.

Some might see that pallid patch,
shaped like a teardrop,as ghost of a past
before the forests came. To me it seemed
living, with its curvy difference
from rows of infant spruce, its very pallor
earthbound light, its unexplained survival
a welcome mystery.

           All those years later,
finding the field still there among grown trees,
still catching the sun down forest rides,
was a kind of happiness, that found a voice
in untranslatable speech of wind
through the uncut hay.

4. New Spell

When conifers first covered these hills, to many
they were the enemy – identity thieves
stealing the character of bare solitudes,
intruding on a perfect relationship
of earth and sky. *Blanket* was the word
often used – *a dark blanket over the hills.*

Looking at this photograph
of an old farm track inside a forest,
and remembering the day I took it, I can't feel
the old hostility.
                              Twenty years and more ago
dry autumn followed the driest of summers.
We'd walked across the lake-bed, its baked mud
a tessellated floor. On the western bank
the forest offered shade and cool.
Firs flanked the track, but ahead the sun
filtered through green-gold sycamore, birch,
above broken walls.
                              In the picture a child,
in red third-birthday wellingtons, is forcing
his breathless way over brashings and stones
to reach the house. There's anticipation, thrill,
in every line of his form.

                                          I remember
surprising myself by sharing a little
of that delight, unprejudiced; that openness
to wonder, where I'd thought to be saddened
by rigidity, spoiling, dull dark, a smothered ruin.
What had seemed nothing but loss
was hiding fresh enclaves of joy. Was a balance
being restored, a new spell woven,
in cool of forests under the acceptant sky?

5. Wild Sheep

Sometimes they are glimpsed
between the trees, a rough
curliness, dingy whiteness,
flicking away with surprising speed –
the wild sheep, the ones gone native
in the forests, unshorn, draggle-tailed.

Never to be espied as restful blobs
on a sweep of grass, they have rejected
pasture as we know it, yet their sturdy breadth
surely means richness of blade and leaf
in ride and secret glade.

They have escaped our pastoral
expectations, unconsciously
compensating with a frisson of the primitive
where we least expected it, spelling out
an aspect of forest we are reluctant
to recognise, a wild hiddenness.

It's as if, defying all that was long the norm
on our unviolated hills; imposed,
unwelcomed, out of character,
the forest find themselves, after all,
subject to a land's dominance, begin
not only to take, but offer.

              There again
a quick slide of movement in the trees,
a hint of savagery where we'd seen
nothing but woolly cliché;
adventure, unpredictability,
finding an unlikely avatar.

Lit Room

It's not dusk yet, though January afternoon
holds the thought of night.
Stone is blackish with damp,
raindrops from the last shower
bead a handrail's underside,
weigh on tiny crocus-points.

Steps rise wetly dark
to an upward-sloping lawn,
half-cloistered, its topmost limit
an unofficial, secret elevation,
the back of the Priory Church, that seems
to feel no need to preach or dominate,
but quietly lies against blank sky,
accepting upward flow of steps and grass,
that can't do other than lead the eye
towards that ancientness and calm.

Right of the climb, ground falls away
to rooftops and roads of the town; beyond,
the mountains rise. To left, a house-wall rears.
Suddenly, inside a tall window high above,
in someone's home an early light comes on.
It's like a surprising chord that clarifies
the music's drift; like the moment when,
as you write, the poem takes over and amazes.

As if looking out from that long window
I turn towards the town below; am conscious now
of thousands of windows that will soon
answer this one's light.
The enclave set apart has still
a usual life flowing within its walls,
sending a light to join so many others.

All seems linked, old solemn stones
above the lawn's intense wet green,
rooftops below, and stir of roads,
new rainy crocuses,distant hills;
this dying day, days to be born,
a neighbourhood, a home.

The Will

He's making his will today.
Our neighbour, skilled in ordering
such matters, guides and writes.
A cluster of cousins crowds round the bed,
not best pleased, I'll warrant,
to find themselves remembered
by a cow here, a small scurry there
of sheep they already pasture.
Our childless state has given them,
as years turned, hopes they are finding
not like to blossom.

His sisters have no need
of much from him, being married
well enough, and never having had
greedy eyes for the down-at-heel farms
that are like to be John's,
his swarthy brother's, now.

As for me, he will make fitting
provision, I have no doubt –
he has always had regard
for form and seemliness, however little
love has sprung from our sober contract.
And, truth to tell, I think I shall not
have a long widowhood, though
of that nor he nor the cousinry
has whisper or inkling.

He has started to cough.
I must scatter the brood of watchers
from the bed, raise him
on his jumbled pillows, mop and dry,
soothe his sweaty brow, hold the cup
to his crusted lips. So near to death
as he is now, the semblance of loving care
will suffice, and of this
I will never cheat him. So now
I will go in.

The Ram

Past the Elderly bungalows –
Not one Elderly
tending a plot, or peeping
between neat curtains.
Silence and cold.

Over the bridge –
the stream's chilly words
neither begin nor end.
They have no aim; nothing
links them to humankind.

Up the lane,
flanking fields are quiet.
Once in a while, sheep bleat.
Seeing me, they huddle edgily
then move away –

except for a formidable ram,
Roman-nosed, male as they come,
who heads for the fence and seems
disposed to fraternise. I scratch
thrusting nose, rough brow,

liking his harsh curly pelt,
meeting the slit stare
of his devil's eyes; and feel
a little warmth in the day,
richness in its quiet.

Joy

At the farm down the road
I remember a sheepdog, lugubrious Joy,
who pensioned off spent her mournful days
drooping in the middle of the road,
meeting with equal indifference
the soothing words of strangers
and the chance of crushing death.

A day came when Joy
disappeared; cars no longer slowed
to dodge the melancholy obstacle.
I couldn't bring myself to ask
Where's Joy?, feeling that while
the question wasn't put,
wasn't answered, I could still
picture her lurking sombrely
in some nook of a barn, even
welcomed inside to eke out
her sad and shortening days
by the stove, or in summer
on the porch mat. It was long
before I accepted the certainty
that never again would Joy's
ineffable dreariness lend
a dark spice to the blandest of days.

Woodpecker

What his tidy black and white
might seem to say
is contradicted by daring red
that flares from nape and rump,
and by repeated stabbing,
fierce, nervous, determined,
of my nut-feeder by his jutting beak.

He would be warm in the hand,
hard and brittle of quill,
soft of breast-feather, sharp
and scrabbly of claw.
That's fantasy. He's well, and wild,
and this respectful distance
is as near as I'll get.

Even to think *my woodpecker*
is unwarranted, cancelled at once
by a flashing-away,
red, black and white vanishing
deep in the trees.

Dreams

1. New Year Dream

Snow lingers at the forest verge
on a fringe of motley trees,
saplings less fragile than they seem,
but dwarfed by tall rigidity of firs,
a middle-ground of disciplined precision.

Further in, dimness, vagueness
at the gate of the year, a place
where figures half-known, wholly strange
are glimpsed and lost: the man
with a faceful of leaves, the snow-girl
with her knife of ice. What light
throws that shadow of horns?

The young year, shivering,
glances over her shoulder
into the duskiness, turns, sets out
for what will be, shaking off doubt
with vestiges of snow, hoping
for simple dark, unambiguous light.
Stark trunks keep the illusion
of biding their time. Far in the dream-forest
a gate swings shut.

2. Landmark

I knew it was the wrong landmark.
The flyover where my road ran
was impossibly high, yet as high
reached up the pearly spire,
fretted, frilly as a thin pagoda,
so near, the perspective
(trick of mist?) was addled, scary.

On this high level everything
was clear-cut, loud, fast.
I had expected to emerge
above the bay, find my way
down to the waterfront.
But below was a grey blur
of street-grids, oddly quiet;
no sign of sea or the shabby grace
of tall hotels from another century's youth.

I thought I must have turned,
and in confusion turned again, reaching,
disconcerted, this height above
an inland edge of the town. I tried
age-old orienteering, searched
overcast sky for a chink of sun.
The delicate climbing spire
had a nacreous gleam; that was all.

How do I get to the harbour? I called.
Two girls smiled at each other, pointed
the way I had come.
I set out, vainly trying
to read a battered sign.
At last came a sense of opening out,
a feeling, again, of height,
a distant greyness – the bay?
But inescapable ahead a filigree shape
printed its delicate dominance on the sky.

3. Threshold

At dawn (so I dreamt),
as I came out of the house,
someone went in.
There was an instant when
each flowed through the other.

Was that an image of my life?-
beginning and end a confluence,
neither stream dominant?
                              Or could it be
that someone destined (unknowing)
to fill my place, had waited
in a knot of trees, perhaps.
or by a broken wall,
till the time came for us to meet
in ignorance, and overlap,
becoming each other once, at dawn?

4. Pale House

Last night I climbed
to a house I knew, shifted five miles
by technology of dream
to a hillside not its own.
A garden spread where none had been, flaunting
June blossom in chill early spring.
Approaching the gate, I glanced aside,
and felt like a cushioned blow
soft shock of an alien presence-
another house, unknown to me,
not far above- simple,in shape foursquare,
yet pale, seeming insubstantial
as if itself a haunting.

'Wise to keep away' I thought at first, but soon
smiled, deprecating such fantasy,
seeing as I climbed nearer
how sturdy and solid was this house,
how welcoming the gold-grey of its stone,
no longer pallid-seeming, no longer vague.

Standing at the window,
I drank the vastness of the view-
down over fields, over little spinneys
and dimmer expanse of marsh beyond,
faintly remembered. In time
I left, unhindered, though I had feared
that might not be allowed. Yet it seems
something, somehow, did suffer change.
In the gold-stone house
some part of me has stayed;
still, in my waking, dream
has its domain.

Threat

Sun and gorse on this forest height.
It's March, but over clearings
there's a faint summery haze,
a trace of scent that later heat
will enrich.

　　　　　To the north
is a movement of ridges
running up into Powys, valleys
green, except for one, black
when cloud or shadow lingers
over conifers dark already.

　　　　　　　　South,
a spread landscape offers
mile after mile of complexity,
stretching itself in these warm
insidious airs. Here and there
a climbing road, cluster of roofs,
river-bend, gleaming in sun,
call to the eye, yet blend
in a pattern that would take
a lifetime to comprehend.

　　　　　　　　Distantly,
dark on the southern skyline,
rises a cleft mountain,
oddly dominant, its very shape
a reminder of cataclysms
that have been and could come again –
a shape as malign, it seems,as a spoken threat.

Far to the south, clouds drift now, mask
that dark horizon. Here on the forest height
shine sun and gorse, March
full of promises, golden light.

Bridges

'That bridge,' he said,
the one you crossed going up the valley –
I built that, rebuilt anyway,
fifteen years ago. There was only
a strip left, not much more
than a tightrope. So I got stones together
(lying around or fallen from bits of wall)
and I built it up. I did the arch
like it had been (yes, it's safe,
guaranteed!) and a parapet each side.
Everyone who comes here(not knowing)
thinks it's the old one. I'm glad of that.
To me it's like I helped the old bridge
not to finish, like it was meant to go on.'

I had stood on the bank, looking up
at his bridge, and seen ancient work,
dark against sun. Could he turn his skills,
I wondered now, to another bridge, downstream,
where only hints remain of bygone bulk,
sturdiness, a confident link
between house and road? There is rock
in the stream-bank; dawdling along,
I saw a grey mass as something made,
a pillar, tucking itself into earth now,
battered and reticent, inside it a tiny room
(privy or wine-store? children's hideaway?)
On the opposite bank, even more hidden,
another pillar of the long-ago bridge.

Not worth the work, he would think, and be right.
Who now would need to cross the stream
to tides of grass and a derelict house?
No romantic whim had made him accept
his bridge-builder's role upstream, but an instinct
for what had not yet run its course, for the dumb
life of the useable unliving thing.
Past the pillars of the dead bridge
goes the pebbly chatter of the stream
with hardly a change of note.

Treachery

It feels nearer the sun up here.
The stony track struggled up
through dark of trees towards
a growing disc of light, which swelled, broke
into majestic brightness.
Now the path levels, the valley opens.

Across the river one farm spreads yard and barns
in shadow against light. Above it rises
bare mountain, a final wall that flanks
the upper valley, curves round its distant head,
in a strange visual accord
with the valley-floor's sharp green
of re-seeded garths, proclaiming
work, settlement, fertility.

Alongside a fence that dwindles
towards the far-off valley-head, unseen
high passes, into barren distance
runs a green road. On it, down
from hidden solitudes, a dark dot
gleams and grows, zooms into a phalanx
of mountain-bikers, black-clad, impassive,
hissing dizzily past. Unmoved,
a fat ewe suckles her twins
under a track-side thorn.

In this domain of sun,
so all-encompassing, so royal,
only the traitor mind creates
in the shiver of sun on skin
a shudder of ice-wind, subverts
with a sly imagining of snow.

Capel-y-Ffin Story

Faces crowded over the boy,
amazed, ecstatic, pleading.
He was frightened by the extreme
emotion, by his new unsought power.

Running down the slope into full sun
he had fallen, lain staring up
into dizzy white of hawthorn,
blue sky a hood above the valley.
Overpowered, his sight
struggled with too great light
that made a visionary strangeness.

It was a valley of stories. They spilled
from the cool-arched monastery
in a tide of visitations and miracles.
Each family hoped for its own marvel.
When he came home dazed, sunstruck,
inarticulate, the prompting questions
began. It grew easier to answer
once he had started. Yes, he said,
yes, it was the Lady, white like fire,
hooded in blue.

When at last he escaped in the cool
to the hillside, he was confused, crying,
heavy with muddled guilt. But soon,
far from the morning's heat,
free from those urgent voices, he felt
in the living air a power
that needed no defining,
posed no questions, only
absolved, mothered, consoled.

Genealogy

1. Census

Census copperplate records her,
the grandmother I couldn't love –
but where's the stormy aunt I liked?
Flown the coop? It caught her later,
that narrow house on a village street;
but when the enumerator counted heads
the only child left was my mother, thirteen,
the youngest, docile and pious, doing a stint
as local monitress, her happy days
at convent-school lying ahead. Even the name
of my formidable granny brings, for once,
a warmth. It's just the thrill
of finding another strand to weave
into my pattern, I know, and yet
perhaps after all these years has come
acceptance, of a sort, as I glimpse
the widow, still young, who had shown
courage, resilience; whose face
in old photographs had surely
some lines of humour. She and I
could hardly help our mutual
antipathy; we were better apart.
But seeing her name recorded here
by a stranger, in a year she lived
long before those uneasily lodged
in my memory, brings a belated
tolerance. No gentle recollection
surfaces, but unexpectedly
I find I wish one could.

2. Black Elm

When I was nine, an envelope
bearing my bachelor uncle's
neat scholarly writing brought
happy anticipation.
A schoolmaster, probably
a good one, he'd always known better
than to write down to me.
                                    But today
was different. He'd sent a story
written specially for me, about
Black Elm.
                        This was a tree
below our house, near the gate –
very tall, and certainly very black
of trunk and branch. My feelings about it
were relentlessly anthropomorphic. To me
it was princely, dangerous, magnetic;
and though my stories of it
never got written down, they were there
in my head, an enriching fantasy
that would have faded in time, but left
a trace of exciting dark.
                              All this my kindly uncle
killed with his little story, of which
not one word can I recall, but know
it had a terrible cosiness. I never
forgave him, though kept a surface
friendliness. I hope he didn't know.

From then on, I'd pass Black Elm
without a glance, without even
feeling a drama of farewell. Easier nowadays
to spot the cut-off points, the endings
that were beginnings, after a fashion,
and after decades hold their hint of pain.

3. Gone Wrong

It was in my grandmother's
orderly house, where nothing extreme
was tolerated, that for the first time
I witnessed a grown-up's real
tempestuous weeping. To this day
I've never known why my aunt
sobbed, rushing up the stairs,
landing boards adding
their creaking plaint, her bedroom door
slamming savagely behind her.

Bored with incomprehensible words
bandied three-handed between
my mother, her sister, their mother
(words that had lit this fuse),
I had noticed little, except a man's name
angrily recurring.
                              No-one explained,
no-one reassured. I remember
feeling shock, a bit of fright,
a lot of puzzlement, and (unusually
for a self-centred child like me) some anger
at an ill-defined unfairness I sensed
my misery-struck aunt had suffered – even
a faint, undeveloped twinge of sympathy,
a dim wish I could set right
something that should have gone well
and had, undeservedly, gone wrong.

4. Compulsion

Sometimes it seems an odd preoccupation,
this clumsy stone-on-stone rebuilding
of broken generations, endless correcting
of the less-than-true. How many treasures
of reminiscence, offered in good faith,
prove to be paste and gimcrack? *Your father
was the fourth of five* – I grew up with that
as a morsel of holy writ, and now, ferreting,
find he was fourth of nine. I had four
small aunts and uncles carried out
boxed in their seemly gowns. After one,
as was the custom, my father was named.

Somehow that brings all those sad midgets
closer, though doesn't explain the strength
of my wish to know. There seems no limit
to the strange sense of kin, that stretches out
beyond the point where grief can be felt,
into a shadowland on the marches of my life –
most of the time ignored, but never
quite to be denied.

Butterflies at Wellfield

Not a dream. The mind's eye,
tranced but unsleeping, held
a magnified fragment of butterfly-wing;
creamy, fluted, its deep brown border
studded with colourless globules,
like drops of rain.
                              So specific,
so meaningless! Calling it back
each time it started to fade, imagining
flowers stirred by summer airs,
courting sensations (once I thought
a powdery brittleness dusted my hand),
trying words for their echoes, I was driven
to the simplest one, *butterfly*.
                              And there it was –
Wellfield, for many childhood years
the empty house next door, tall and white,
standing alone at the top of a grassy slope
that was lawn once, but known to me
as flowery meadow misted with coloured clouds
of butterflies, and moths almost as bright,
that I spent hours netting, to brood over,
let go.
                  I can't remember
The cream-and-brown one. That's as it should be.
The big house, a puzzle and provocation
to my friends and me, who dared sometimes
to explore, rushing out at half-heard sounds,
unexplained; the sweep of meadow
with its coloured clouds of petals and wings –
right that its last haunting of my mind
should be baffling, this glimpse
of an uncatchable wing.

Garlanding the Urn

This lady in bas-relief
seems to be cuddling an urn
almost as tall as herself.
Her rounded arms emerge
from draperies enveloping
but nearly transparent
to enfold the unresponsive
object of her solicitude.
On closer inspection, one sees
she is setting around it
a garland of flowers; her expression
gives nothing away.

She is an unexpected sight
on a kitchen wall, surmounting
not carved eulogy,genealogical
trumpeting, but a row
of little flasks and jars; and close
neighbour to saucepan-shelf,
cooker and fridge. She's not alone –
random tablets proclaim
that somewhere underneath us lie
remains of worthies of the parish
whose church became this house.

An unlikely marriage, but not perhaps
unhappy; an acceptant union
of what was with what is – something
of the macabre, a touch of humour,
a continuing celebration (in the main
unconscious) of those far-off Parrys
and Morrises whose bones
are crumbling peacefully to dust
beneath our feet; and on the wall
an urn forever garlanded.

Eyes

A word here and there
struggles to emerge
from fractures, blotches, peeling,
discolouration. I think
the bones that lie beneath this stone
belonged to one Rhys Jones. I'm sure
of nothing.
                    At the top of the stone a few
small decorations could be dangling flowers
or maybe bells, flanking
a lighter, larger blob.
                            I turn to go
but look back, feeling, oddly,
I may have missed the point – and meet,
from that central shape, the straight searching look
of two eyes, shockingly alive.
                                    Thick-nosed,
slit-mouthed, now the face reveals itself;
and the eyes live as nothing else
in the whole God's Acre manages to do.

What sculptor, what client chose
from possible patterns, instead
of doves or flowers, bland cherubs, urns, harps,
this face with its challenging stare?
How did a rural craftsman know
the trick of giving such luminosity,
such judging intelligence, to a pair of eyes?

                        Somehow it seems
appropriate that on the flaking stone,
surmounting vague patterns of decay,
there should remain a seeking mind,
still questioning, still making its demands,
confronting us, from these carved eyes.

Time and the Running Child

More ancestors! laughed the visiting child,
running down a staircase flanked by portraits.
She thought the gothic grandeur of her friend's home
entertaining. The cramped ladder-like steps to servants' rooms
of another century tempted her to explore;perhaps now,
remembering, she finds in her mind's lumber-room
unalarming ghosts, long-skirted girls in a perilous rush,
squeezing down to answer a distant demanding bell.

Child's laughter, clatter of running feet on polished wood,
muted in carpeted hall – then through the porch and out.
The gargoyled house behind her was strange enough,
full enough of unpredictable treasures, to keep her
on happy tenterhooks. This was her first sense
of the heady past, now spelt out, now hinted, the way it mixed
with beginnings, with that moment as she ran out,
weeks of holiday stretching ahead, and over horizon hills
blue sky, unfathomable, endless.

Swallow Leaving

Taking linen upstairs, I found
a swallow in my room. Quickly
I shut us in, lest it should find
a whole house to get lost in.
It didn't panic; its fluttering
seemed leisurely, a soft movement
in irregular curves. But it ignored
the open window, preferring height to light,
staying where the loftier ceiling had, perhaps,
the reassurance of sky.
                          How to coax it
towards deliverance? I moved nearer,
speaking quietly, hoping my presence might seem
something to avoid, might gently chivvy the bird
to the bright opening that meant escape
into real sky, buoyant currents of air.

It perched on a picture-frame, letting me
have a moment or two to savour
precision of slenderness, touch of rich colour;
then resumed that weaving flight around
the wrong end of the room, passing close above me,
seemingly unafraid. Surely to the swallow
I was just another object below, this one
moving, at times emitting a sound,
but mattering no more than bed or chair.

What was the reason
for its choice of the moment to leave?
It went flitting, this time faster, dipping to the window,
and with a wing-beat was gone, giving itself
to the lifting energy of spring air,
mile after unconfined mile.
                            I crossed
the empty room, and opened the door.

Homecoming

They were so disappointed. They knew
the name of the family farm
and where it stood,
but when they climbed up the track
there was nothing to see,
only a shelf of hill.

Whatever makes a pope
kiss the ground, a conqueror
humble himself before
a handful of earth,
didn't work for them.
They'd wanted something
of what a forebear had made
and link-generations had kept or changed,
loved, been irked by, or simply
taken for granted – the shell
in which the secret, vulnerable
family-creature had lurked.

Here, they found nothing to recognise,
nothing to claim them, nothing
to belong to. There seemed no point
in staying to hear wind in the grass,
watch cloud skim the hill, let the eye
follow an ancient path down to the stream.

Nursing bafflement, dissatisfaction,
they turned away, with no notion
that with footfall after footfall
over generations, their brief
dismissive tread would be part for ever
of the ground of home.

Wrecker and Roaring Saint

for my great-great-grandfather, Hannibal Richards

Weather rhyme – March saints.
first comes David, then comes Chad,
then comes Winnol, roaring like mad.

It was May, though, and quiet weather,
when the small procession came to Winnol's church –
father, Christian the mother with her bundled baby;
and the godsibbs, to speak the words of rejection
that would discomfort the fiend,
and the words of embracement
to give the child Christ's mark.
                                          Sand was hot,
pressing close to the church on the beach;
baptismal water cool comfort, no shiver or shock.
Many-named Winnol, Winwalloe, Guénolé,
remember the child.

He made no sound. His eyes hadn't changed yet
from infancy's blue. Come March gales,
there'd be dark in his looks and his cries
to answer Winnol's roars. Another year,
he'd be staggering over the sand,
kicking and yelling when plucked
from the frothy verge of tall waves.
Winwalloe, Guénolé, remember the child.

And the man he would grow to? One of many on whom
the sea-devil set his claws, the devil
come rolling in on the back of a wave,
and scrabbling from hold to hold on the slippery cliff.
One of many, but this man a leader –
beyond others daring, skilled, happy in the dark work.

Was nothing of innocence left? Not in small joys he had –
foam's caress, or gale getting up,
prising at windows and eaves?
Not in a grudge let go? In thieves' honour?
Not in a laugh, as he swung to his shoulder
a badgering child? Not in love?
Roaring Winnol, Winwalloe, Guénolé,
remember him,
remember the boy on the beach.

To the Fish Traps

One in four
up the Devil's Staircase, but a full car
labours today; we could swear
it's one in three on these savage twists.
The least nervous might picture
a dizzy slip-back, road and sky
crazily spinning in lethal reverse.

It's hot! Down, down.
'Let's go to the Fish Traps'.
We head for the Tywi, park
in dimness of firs.
Bypassing barriers, we climb and crawl
to savour the river's cool.

By concrete walls
of the Fish Traps, rises the Lime Tower.
Under the chain, up the clanging steps,
peer from the bit of balcony. Upstream,
heat hasn't stinted grass. Between
river and trees it's heavy and deep.
Just seen, a remnant of walls – Cwmdu,
where Harries preached glory, love and fire,
and 'Glory!' his hearers shouted back.

Tower and ruined house
confront each other over an acre of grass;
two thought-shapes over years of change.
Past the stones of Cwmdu,
beyond forests grown, forests felled,
stretch the *blaenau*:
                        through it all
a living homeness, like blood, like breath.

Set Free

1

It would have taken too long
to walk round the lake. We turned back
at the bridge near the heronry,
where long beaky shapes sailed the sky.

Better this way – though, given time,
on such a benign day we'd have gone on,
looping the promontory, catching and losing
sun or water through trees, gone right round
to the start, and all those birds there – scores of them,
pressing in to be fed: stolid Brent geese
heavily plashing in shallows,
a greed of ducks eagerly chugging inshore,
outermost a solemnity of swans.

But better like this: a whole domain
only guessed at – glitter and sway, depths clear
or fronded with weed; leaf-scents, old paths;
none of it certain, none of it captive, all set free
to ghost what we kept of the day.

2

He's a long way off. I can't make out
the white creatures advancing
just ahead of his feet. When he gets near,
they translate, strangely, as doves,
six of them, heads thrust forward, jerked back,
gait a smoothed out shuffle.
You look like a shepherd! I call,
and we both start to laugh, because
that's what he was, in the days of work.

The doves take exception to laughter;
flow on to the road, miraculously
escaping two cars and a lorry.
Reaching the safety of grass,
they are suddenly airborne,
spiralling disdainfully above us,
above rooftops and trees, dwindling
between hills, freeing us
from dailiness, lifting us
into a vision of wings.

3

There are places whose nature seems
random, bitty, humorous even,
like this patch, (hardly a field)
I'm passing, close to the small train.

It's fenced, each side, with wobbly pales;
behind sprout the back-kitchens
of tenements. I'm surprised
by colour. Certainly the grass,
surviving in flattened lumps,
isn't really green. Yet the litter
is cheerful – squashed plastic buckets
minus handle, shouting red;
rich rust of metallic debris, grass
weaving in and out of struts and rods.

Backing it all, those houses. They've been
colour-washed, once, all different –
blue, pink, yellow, one a kind of
half-hearted purple – and now
are faded, peeling, but still have an echo
of care for the eye's delight.

As the little diesel crawls by
I'm left with a sense of something
damaged, but laughing; something
fragmentary, but adding up
to a livelier identity than you'd find
in sober, tidy streets of the hinterland.

No-one expected much
of this almost-field –
it's free of that burden,
free to be its own
scruffy insouciant self,
free to display its art
of quirky celebration.

4

I remember a bend
in an unfamiliar road,
patchy colours of a wall,
the angle of a house
by a stunted tree –
all snatching at my mind
as I passed.

           There were no links
with my life, no giggling or tears
of long-gone children, no pandemonium
of the heart. Yet something brushed by,
uninvolved in any memory of mine,
free to wake a sudden sense
of the parallel, unpredictable, free
to let me catch from far the tiny clear
bell-song of the unexplained.

5

...the truth shall make you free:
what frees me *is* my truth –
a long lane climbing out of twisted oaks,
above the curling tumble of a stream,
into the hills. Not possible to see
any time, any out-of-time moment,
when I won't be part of this.
I'm shackled by air and grace,
my truth a fettered freedom,
my day eternity.

Looms

The way lies along a lawn,
down a mown green lane,
through fields where buttercups today
hold globules of rain
over a stream, up slithery steps
and the hill beyond.
                     In the copse
that darkly caps it,, there's a glimpse
of stone. Above mist,
at the high centre of this round valley,
appears through branches a small church,
grass trimmed round a scatter of graves.

Inside, a swept floor, polished wood,
harmony and care. To see, nothing
unforgettable. Little to hear,
only the soft breath of rain. But felt
as soon as the door opens,
beyond all expectation,
is power, as if in this place
great silent looms are running, running,
endlessly working, shaping, enhancing,
endlessly mending the rents in torn lives.

We shall stay
though we shut the door,
go out into thickening rain,
turn away.

All Manner of Thing

There was no-one to be seen.
The long lane led to silent houses,
an ancient garden-wall straggled over
by greenery, red-lit by apples – all still,
all plunged into midday depth,
fullness, of sun.
                              Stone steps into shade
felt like movement waking, as they climbed
to the churchyard's wide sunny circle
bordered by shadow, aged graves aslant
as if tipping into sleep – and at last
soft sound – swish and clink of an unseen river
in trees below sanctuary at the silent church.

This place, forgotten in a wrinkle
of a small country's mountains, felt
as though it could hold encircled the life,
through millennia after millennia, of a world.
Tectonic plates had shiggled and slid,
continents parted and joined, ice ages come and gone.
A long-dying sun burning on towards doom
seemed here in September to cherish
and be cherished.
Like the whisk of warm grass on skin
a hardly-formed thought brushed by –
might everything so embraced
indeed, ultimately, be well?

Rainbow

Llanfair Cilgeddin

The church is disused, not derelict;
corners of notices in the porch
curl as the print fades. Locked inside
are wall-paintings – the key-holder's away.
On tiptoe outside a window one can catch
pictured curves of rainbow and hill.

This is a place of quiet, but not of peace.
Something here disturbs with a sad
ambivalence. Rough-mown, the churchyard
has islands of wilderness, where tombstones
rise out of tangle, their names
festooned, prickled, obscured.

But over there, rigidly railed in,
a dozen graves or more, with no
visible names, enigmatically
break the pattern, seeming to attempt
order, definiteness, in this acre of doubt,
yet keep their secrets.

The railings are tall; their blotched
rusting spikes, blade-shaped,
menace the sky, reach towards
a snarl of trees, one dead, the weird
contortions of its silvery branches
held up or strangled by battening holly.

Can anything unhallow
what was once consecrated? It seems
a savagery, never perhaps
wholly suppressed, has broken through.

Bells fell silent, music faded
into leaf-stir, long faint water-talk
from a distant river-bend.
Wisps of smoke from the last snuffed candles
curled away. The dark grew strong,
at noon no less than dead of night. Who now
stabs and slashes with a sword of prayer?

And yet through dusty days, on inner walls
children play, winged winds of heaven dance,
hills keep their certainties, the rainbow triumphs;
and still, for this, sometimes the people come.

Dance

Anything could be read into the shapes
of this weird wood – anything
but happiness, tranquillity.
By the track, two little trees
set-to-partner, each
grotesquely matching the other's
angles and ccurves. Beyond,
score on score up the slope
writhe naked oaks, stunted, pale.
Yet they dance, they dance,
obedient to the day's nature, the swirl
and pulse of hidden waters
under God's Well, the wheeling
of seven great birds – kites who now
after brief vanishing to some other
fastness have silently returned
as though to complete their figure
in the inclusive dance, lazily mounting
spiral stairs of air to circle
against rich blue above
the Well of God, the sunny hill.

Wind in Sumac

Sumac and wind have made a man
in a frondy wide-legged suit,
and suspended him over blown grass.

His beaky head turns this way and that,
looking here, there, for what? It seems
he tries to clap his leafy hands,
manages just an unintelligible
gesture.
        One's not certain
if he's happy – sometimes his head sinks;
what looked like a dance may be
a desperate fit of shaking. The wind is stronger;
perhaps he knows he can't defy it.

But a sudden updraught blows
his frondy limbs skywards; willy-nilly
he flings up his head, confronts
wind, cloud, thunder threat,
with what is surely defiance,
surely, at last, delight.

Diptych, Generation Gaps

1. Before the Dark

He wants his hour before the dark, they said,
knowing and tolerant. Tomorrow he,
the prudent one, who'd added field to field,
the envied one, who never yet shared his hearth,
but now could feel a tightening of the rope
death held him on, would marry a girl,
an all-but-child.
                              Fifteen, she was,
and beautiful, her birthday a week ago.
And how, they asked, had that been squared?
– the contract made by a minister of God,
the signing and sealing complete? Only he,
surely, could have driven that through.

I think that evening, as the sun sank,
he might have stood on the high track
above the farm, and looked down at the house
that he would make her home for the little time
he'd craved since he first set eyes on her.

Powerful as lust, and more insidious,
had come a deep disturbance of the spirit,
incomprehensible and wild,
as if he'd had nothing all his life,
since she had not been in it –
been landless, unskilled, had no sense
of coming weather or an animal's
impending difficult birth; as if he'd been
always unhandy, weak, a mawkish failure
at every enterprise. It seemed
that only she, this girl, this hardly more than child,
could make him whole.

                        He hardly knew her,
had little notion how to wake in her
love or its faintest likeness. Yet
tomorrow she would come. Now
last sunlight stroked his empty house.
Stumbling a little, he made his way
home, knowing there, so soon, was to begin
his hour before the dark.

2. Reading Yeats in September

The old farmyard is grassed over.
In benign sun he lies naked,
his head in her lap. Small September wind
warmly riffles her skirt.

She reads him 'The Cloths of Heaven'.
Half asleep, he stretches a hand
to touch hers; for a moment the book
trembles.
             Generations divide them –
for her, September may not come again.
Today that is almost forgotten;
There is only sun in its kindliest mode,
the little breeze with no hint of chill.

He slides into sleep. She lays down the book,
strokes his hair. Now she sees
that a night and a day can be a life,
and life be never-ending.

Driving Home

A July day, but unseasonable. The city
gleamed grey. Rain turned roads
and pavements to shallow streams
rippling in sneaky wind.

Late on the homeward drive, the day woke.
Over to the west, hills were black
on a livid sky. Now
sunset exploded over the valley. Illusion
of huddled hedges, crouching hills
was gone. Now dizziness
of low light blinded us
with multifaceted shine.
                                    The countryside
grew complex – every leaf, twig, blade, petal
brightly outlined – yet simple in oneness
of ecstasy. Landscape
was love, was joy, the fiery change
a gift that could not be refused
or die with the creeping dark.

At Capel-y-Ffin

suggested by a painting by Edgar Holloway

The gate slants one way, church another.
Sky's black, churchyard
apocalyptically shining.
Slab tombs tip-tilt; at any moment
the risen dead may break into dance
under the yews, under the lift,
spread, beat of seraphim's wings.

This is the moment after which
nothing can be the same;
when love rips through a life,
when a world bursts forth, when chaos
begins its improbable rule.

Birds Returning

Across the meadow an ash tree
had its leaves at last.
Decked for short summer in delicate green, it reached
high on a backdrop of thunderheads.

Blackly silhouetted, a whirl of birds
invaded the boughs, but not for long.
A couple took wing, a little group, then all were gone.

Illogically saddened, I read
the runes of flight and got no answer,
only a heaviness of the heart
acknowledging loss – until

between dark land and threatening cloud
there slid a band of greenish sky,
weirdly resplendent.

One by one, in clusters, then suddenly
thronging, came birds to crowd the tree,
green radiance dancing over
a hundred flittering flickering shapes that spelt
the joy of unlooked-for light.

Elan in Autumn

Hardly the faintest autumn chill
under warm skin of halcyon weather
announces the season on these bare hills.
Sleek, sun-gold, they stretch away.
Man-made lakes take the sky's blue,
adding their own intensity.

               A tiny ruined shop
is strangely alone on a distant slope.
Downstream, drawn on the waste,
is the square of a Roman fort.
Perched above a dam, that house,
with expansive windows proudly set
to display the prospect, is younger
by centuries than its site.
                     Time and time
are gathered up with no confusion,
no separation but that of quiet miles
beneath a seasonless inclusive sun.

Rhaeadr Castle

Imagine walls
tall and dark on top of the hill.
Imagine the fortress, build it
from the nothing it has been
for centuries. Then dissolve it
into this day, this grassy plateau
(not one stone on another).
A dog-leg path leads down to the river;
in heavy shade of stooping trees
a feeder-stream throws its water-notes
into the Wye's plashy talk-and-talk flow.

Now – the unseizable phantom –
is what the river insists on,
with its clichés of oneness. Mind
sees what it chooses, what eye fails at –
the gone walls rising, the halls that were.

October Light

to Harry

By chance I have come to a place
of heights and depths, where depth
is healing as height,
and late in a froward season
today seems blest.

Out of shade into hazy sun
mass and climb blossoming shrubs,
redly glowing, and trees that have lost
hardly a leaf. Behind them,
just caught against sun, is a glimpse
of thin towers.
                          Beside a green track,
branchily arched, there's a drop
through tangle and shafts of light
down, down to silvery curdle of river.

Pausing, I feel by my foot a stir
in debris of twigs and old leaves –
a baby squirrel, sturdy but helpless, lost,
its little strength, like its future,
as nothing. My camera's flash
turns it in less than a second
to a rippling white ghost.

My day is shadowed by your night;
I have no skills for doctoring the dark.
But I will send you a moment of stillness
from this place of ambiguous beauty
that can't exclude pain,
can't reverse loss, yet seems
to take us into the arms of light.

Links

Late now
for a new vision, yet however veiled,
however partial, one has come.

1. Entanglement

I can't remember
my harassed, hostile physics master
mentioning *entanglement* – the tiny particles
that interact, then separate,
still seeming, though far apart, to know
once and for ever each its endless twin,
its partner in the dance, mirroring across
depth and distance every shift and spin.

Entanglement – that oddly poetic term
might well have caught my wandering thoughts,
hinted at a mystery worth exploring,
connected with all that filled a youthful mind:
love, mostly, love and loss, the way a twitch
on one mind tweaks another, miles away.

I might have thought I understood
how the relationship cohered
while *secret from the rest of the world* –
a physicist's words; but it's not a concept
that could have warmly breathed
in our stark laboratory, where dust-motes
loaded reluctant rays of sun.

2. Weather Forecast

When you were young, weather was for using,
a backdrop to imagined scenes –
sun-splinters in lake water, the two of you
lazing on the shore: dark shelter at the core of storm.
Apart, you shared the same sky
with its unpredictable gifts, making links across miles.

You may think the years have broken those bonds.
Now, it seems, storm-wind or quiet air, dryness or wet,
are that and no more. Are you sure? On the radio,
area forecasts; a city's name catches you – *temperature
disappointing, frequent showers.* Can you say you never
wonder if he's walking through the rain?

3. Linked

When my mind makes pictures with no provenance,
happenings unplaced, no memories of mine,
sometimes it's as if they have reached me
from a mind whose dark waves
make me feel their uneasy flow.

There can be only assent. Yes, unknowing
give me your memories to gentle,
to smooth the sharpness that cut you,
to absorb the hurt.
     When I have pictured
a calm sea, there is your boat, waiting.

Film Ending

At the film's end a couple walked away
into the town, his hand on her shoulder,
in friendly silence. Moving easily
they receded, becoming hard to separate
from scores of others who dawdled or hurried by –
a merging of lives that seemed
hope and validation.
A calm ending; but the heart
builds connections beyond logic,
surprises with unshed tears.

Bethlehem

Long reaches of flooded Tywi
are silver-blue in December sun,
bare hedgerow trees pale gold, high fields
clear green, lower ones by water's edge
dank greenish-brown. In southern distance
lovely Llandeilo, climbing its hill,
rises up crested with trees.
                    We are high and dry
on the back road through Bethlehem. Soon
bundle after bundle of Christmas cards
will be brought for the coveted postmark.
What more than a name can be the gift
of such make-believe? Nothing, I've thought,
dismissive of passing cars, muffled travellers
who smiling cram more clutches of cards
into the bursting box.
                    Make-believe too
in that far-off namesake – for *little town*
read *turbulent city*; where in all that mistrust
is the *dreamless sleep* so gently hymned?

And yet today, with winter light playing
over riverine land, gold-wire trees,
the town gracing its shapely hill, I feel
more unity than incongruity. Now,
gifts of the ancient story coincide
with gifts of this day, this landscape,
this fortunate weather. It's a name
that holds them, seeming as valid here as far,
as close and safe a home for dreams
of unfailing reconciliation.

More of the Same

Snow on the field, frost on the trees
are no less beautiful now I am tired
of white glare – same field, same trees,
from the same window, same room
where I am penned by a megrim
and ice underfoot. The traffic can freely roll
on the black salted road, but walkers
go pecking and slithering
on uncleared ruts of the freeze.

In the warm room the radio
drones on – snow down, snow to come,
temperatures on an icy slide,
more of the same, more of the same.

Icicles on the fence don't drip –
they stay shapely, triumphant,
beautiful, catching a ray
of ineffectual sun, beautiful
when fog comes over, and they
are the last visible shapes
before acres of formless grey.

I will turn my back. There shall be
no *eye of beholder* – where
is rejected beauty now?
peevishly I ask, and turn away.

Harmony

Christmas Day. We are out at last,
joining the sunny song
of a cleared road under our wheels.
On either hand tall trees,
bright silver against blue sky, sweep on
diminuendo into distance.

When in longed-for spring
or the still heat of summer
I hear as I always do an undersong,
let it not be discord of treacherous ice,
fog or smirched snow, but this
ethereal triumphant line
of winter music, completing
the year's harmony – singing, singing.

Tout Passe

Patricio, August 2011

Sheltering in the porch
on a grey August morning with wind
bitter as unfriendly autumn, I feel
more hope than on many a soft day
of summer illusion, more trust
than is often mine –
                    born, perhaps
of the nature of this place, its air
of promises kept for centuries,
promises to be kept always,
even if the church fell piecemeal,
the great chancel-screen
rotted and crumbled,
the prized altars of stone were left
with no roof to protect them,
buffeted by gales, draped
in altar-cloths of snow.

A day may come
with little to be seen but hill,
trees, grass, random stone,
as when the story began.

Promises, hope. Yet
the centuries rolling,
the small things of my life,
its laughter, its loves, passing
on the surge of a chill wind.

Tout passe, tout casse, tout lasse.
No. Not everything. Not here.

House By The Ford

1. Noon

We wander along the hot river-bank,
envying the frolicking dogs, who in midstream
are content with shadeless noon, suffering
no torpor or dazzle, begging only
for sticks to be thrown, happily spending
their limitless energy.

The solitary house by the ford
was never ordinary (so the stories hint).
Who lived here? There was the old atheist,
staunch in disbelief in Revival days,
untouched by the frenzy or the glow.
There were the brother and sister,
farming into their nineties here,
with little help, no need for company
outside their tight exclusive bonding.

And in our time, those who come here
from a too different world
with too much confidence, too easy hope,
suffer a sad erosion of their dream
by solitude, darkness, deluge, bleakest winter.
They find a land can make no compromise,
being what it is, insentient. They are alone
with oil-lamps' shallow light, never enough
to neutralise such depth of shadow.
Their mobiles vainly struggle for a signal,
mute against daunting hills.
The narrow switchback road is one
snow-ploughs abandon first, leaving
the distant house unreachable, its dwellers far
from safety of mind or any reassurance
of neighbourhood, and prey to more
than they had ever imagined.

Today we have summer noon, unclouded sun.
We're as unchallenged, uninvolved
as the romping dogs, who shower us
with cool droplets shaken from wet pelts.
That, perhaps – that carefree energy,
sunny playfulness – is what we'll take home
to sum the day: not a last glimpse of the house
across the ford in dark of trees;
not stir of boughs in a small wind
out of nowhere, when all the air
had seemed still; not that odd sense of questions
unclear, unhopeful of answers.

2. Picnic

Three women picnicking by the stream
laugh to find themselves here, on stony grass,
with autumn new and the wind sharp.

Under faded grass, under shallow soil,
rock.
Under words, laughter, the stream's clatter,
silence.

Across the ford, trees toss, half-hiding
a grey house; its owner has gone wandering.
Today no sun freckles walls with shadows of leaf.

Under the trees' wild surging,
stillness.
Under sadness of leaving, intimation
of return.

3. The Glade

From down by the ford
the hill looks flattened, smaller,
with the tall trees felled.
Not for ever. The forest-cycle holds
clearing, replanting, upspringing –
thirty years or so of growth,
new hiddenness, encroaching dark, before
the midget figures and their bright machines
lay all low, make for a while
a foreground of stubbly chaos, a distance
of folded hills. We greet forgotten vistas
with uncertain, conditional delight,
knowing next time we lose them, loss
will for us be final.

The house across the stream
has in its name *Llanerch,* glade. The word
reaches back and back to a forest
not man-contrived, not subject
to rhythms man ordained,
yet in the end, whether felled or burned
or shrivelling in a tree-plague, becoming
less than a memory – rumour, question
for map-makers, echo in a name. Still
there is the feeling here of a place
opened, cut from wilderness
to admit, precariously, the idea of home.

The solitary house has its own sheltering spinney.
There will be some, passing through,
who in its sighing dark will fancy
echoes of ephemeral forests
on hills beyond, or think they sense
shadows and faintest crepitation
of wind in the ancient woods
that must have seemed eternal;
then, driving up the dizzy road
to plateau-land, will head
for treeless coast and open skies.

Notes

To the Fish Traps:

Fish traps were usually built for collecting the eggs of salmon and sea-trout.

Lime is fed into the Tywi river above Llyn Brianne reservoir to counteract the acid of coniferous forests.

The area is associated with the 18th-century evangelising of Howell Harries.

blaenau -uplands where rivers rise

Generation Gaps: 1. Before the Dark

In 1809 an Abergwesyn farmer married a girl of 15.

The character in the poem is fictional.

The phrase about the hour before dark I heard used in Abergwesyn in the 1970s.